This book is dedicated to my wife Lynelle, for understanding and supporting the call on my life as a First Response Chaplain. Her love, patience, and support have carried us through this journey!

Hope Offered

On the Worst Possible Day of Someone's Life...Hope

Those men and women who serve their communities as Police, Fire, or EMS Chaplains are subjected to traumatic scenes and crisis settings that most individuals will never see. Because they are exposed to the same scenes and settings as First Response personnel, Chaplains also need to be encouraged and built up in their faith. This devotional has multiple purposes: To build up the Chaplain's faith and hope, to be utilized as a tool to minister proactively with First Responders and, to offer hope on the worst possible day of someone's life....

Introduction

It's not IF...
It's WHEN...

Crisis is going to come and
Chaplains will be in the middle of it.

This booklet is designed for First Response
Chaplains to use as a daily devotional. In the pages
ahead, Chaplains can draw from Christian
Scriptures to strengthen their walk and calling.
They can also use these verses with those who are
caught in the middle of trauma, crisis, and
hopelessness.

Day 1

Joy in Believing...

"And may the God of hope fill you with all joy and peace in believing, that you may abound in hope through the power of the Holy Spirit"
(Rom 15:13 MKJV)

Our God is THE God of hope. He is the object, the author, and foundation on which our hope is built. As we lean on and lead others to the God of hope, we and they have the opportunity to be filled with joy and peace simply by believing - by placing trust and faith in the God of hope. And as we step out in faith, this scripture promises that we may have an overflowing abundance of hope not through our own strength or abilities, but through the power of the same Holy Spirit that raised Jesus from the grave.

The more we place our hope in the God of hope, the more joy and peace we will have because our faith will grow stronger. We should desire and be driven to seek an abundance of hope.

Prayer

Father,

I come boldly before Your throne today and I worship you as the God of hope. I place my faith in Your ability to bring joy and peace in my life. I trust in the promise of Your word and by faith, I embrace the joy and peace that I receive from You, THE God of hope.

In Your Name I pray.

Day 2

Hurry Up & Wait...

"But those who wait on Jehovah shall renew their strength; they shall mount up with wings as eagles; they shall run, and not be weary; they shall walk and not faint" (Is 40:31MKJV)

We've probably all heard the saying, "Hurry up and wait". So often we're impatient and confident in our own sufficiency and strength that we jump in with both feet and end up burned out, frustrated, and unable to come to a satisfactory conclusion to our situation. In a time of crisis, we often want to be the hero and "fix it" ourselves. But this particular scripture reveals God's way of walking through the circumstances in front of us: We wait. One of the most difficult things we can willingly do when we know something needs to be done. But if we wait, our strength will be made new AND we will not get exhausted nor will we faint. We WILL get through whatever crisis or circumstance we face.

Waiting: To look for, to hope, to expect. Choose to wait!

Prayer

Father,

Thank You for the promise in Isaiah 40:31. Thank You that You SHALL renew my strength if I will simply choose to wait on You. Thank You that I will not get exhausted, that I will not grow weary and that I will get through this circumstance by Your strength renewed in me!

In Your Name I pray.

Day 3

I've Got a Plan…

"For I know the plans I have for you, declares the LORD, plans for welfare and not for evil, to give you a future and a hope"
(Jer 29:11 ESV)

Think about this for a moment: God knows you by name. He knows you personally. Think about this as well - The Creator of the universe has plans for you and He knows what they are and their outcome!

Too often we don't know what to think about a given situation. Especially in the time of trauma or crisis! Our thoughts are often jumbled and we're not quite sure what to do or what the outcome will be. God's plans for us are for our good. They are not designed to harm us. His outcome for us is for us to have a future and a hope!

Prayer

God,

You have a plan for me! I am awestruck that You, the Creator of the universe, know who I am and if I will place my trust and hope in You, You will bring me through any and every circumstance that I will face, and that Your plans and thoughts for me will bring me peace   hope. Thank You, Father for Your plan for my life.

In Your Name I pray.

Day 4

I Am, I Will...

"Do not fear; for I am with you; be not dismayed; for I am your God. I will make you strong; yes, I will help you; yes, I will uphold you with the right hand of My righteousness" (Isaiah 41:10 MKJV)

This verse really speaks about silencing our fears. It encourages us to exercise our faith and hope in God in times of distress. This particular verse begins with, "Do not fear". That isn't a suggestion, that's a command! Because God Himself is saying directly to you, "I am" and "I will", you can look fear in the face and refuse to bow your knee to it! God says:

"I am with you; I am your God" - That means that He will never leave us! Not only is He always with us, He is OUR God!

"I will make you strong; I will help you; I will uphold you with My righteousness" - God promises that He will make us strong, that He will help us through our situation, and that He Himself will support and keep us in His right hand of justice!

Prayer

Father,

Thank You for always being with me! Thank You for being my God. Thank you for making me strong, for helping me, and for supporting me in Your hand of justice! I place my hope in You!

In Your Name I pray.

Day 5

Praise, Patience, & Prayer…

"Rejoicing in hope, patient in affliction, steadfastly continuing in prayer" (Rom 12:12 MKJV)

We honor God by placing our hope and trust in Him, especially when we purposefully rejoice in that hope, when we put our confidence in His word and His promises towards us.

We are to be patient in difficult times. We are able to bear bravely and calmly what we must walk through. If we take the time to strengthen placing our hope and trust in Him when we're not in crisis, we are more likely to be patient and sit at His feet during times of trauma or crisis.

The anchor of developing our hope and trust is to lay a firm foundation of fervent and perseverant prayer. Without the intimate, personal communication with God, we will never be able to whole-heartedly place our hope and trust in Him.

Prayer

Father,

I rejoice in the hope You have given me! I rejoice in the fact that I can place my trust in You because You have shown Yourself over and over and over to me through Your faithfulness to fulfill the promises in Your Word. Thank you for the opportunity to sit at Your feet in times of trouble, to lay beside still waters in the presence of crisis and trauma.

In Your Name I pray.

Day 6

Where Did I Put That?…

"And now, Lord, what do I wait for? My hope is in You" (Ps 39:7 MKJV)

This verse speaks of placing our hope in the proper place. We have to ask ourselves, "Where did I put that? Where is my hope?"

So often we place our hope and trust in the things of this world- friends, relatives, doctors, lawyers, and the list goes on. We sit back and we expect mankind to offer us THE solution to our situation, and when those solutions don't work, we don't know where to turn.

David asks the question in this verse, "What am I waiting for?" The he follows up with an incredible statement: "My hope is in You!". David knew where he put his hope. He knew the solution to his problem. We have to have that same confidence, that same assurance that David did. We have to KNOW that we put our hope in God.

Prayer

Father,

Strengthen my faith today. Strengthen my hope and my confidence in Your promises towards me. I choose to place my trust in You and not in the things of this world. I choose to place my hope and trust in You.

In Your Name I pray.

Day 7

In Witness Protection…

"You are my hiding place and my shield; I hope in Your Word"
(Ps 119:114 MKJV)

Witness Protection is the protection, or safe-keeping of a witness involved in a situation that is dangerous to them. They may even be given a new identity and live the rest of their lives under the guidance, direction, and support of a governmental authority.

Those in witness protection are often placed in a safe house with alarms and protection. Our "safe house" is God Himself. He is our hiding place. He is our shield. Think of a SWAT Team breaching a door. The point on the team usually carries a shield that protects the people behind him from being injured or killed. God, as our shield quenches every fiery dart the enemy can throw!

In times of crisis, we can hide in the shadow of His wing; we can enter the witness protection program and place our hope and trust in His Word.

Prayer

Father,

Thank You for protecting me day in and day out. Thank you for being my shield and my hiding place! Thank you that during times of crisis I can place my trust in You to protect me.

In Your Name I pray.

I Hope So…

"But I will hope without ceasing, and I will add more in all Your praise" (Ps 71:14 MKJV)

In this verse, David's fears are silenced. In the midst of trouble and enemies plotting against him, he chooses to offer praise and thanksgiving. David states that he will 'hope without ceasing". What does that mean to hope without ceasing?

How can David do that? Because he has placed his hope and trust in the strength of God (verse 16).

To be able to constantly and continually place our hope in God's strength and not our own will cause us to speak of His love and care for us as we praise Him more and more for what He is doing for us in times of crisis and need.

Prayer

Father,

When I have said all I can say to glorify You, I know that there is more to be said! As I go forth speaking of Your love and care for me, I will constantly and continuously place my hope and trust in You. No matter the circumstance Lord, I place my hope and trust in You.

In Your Name I pray.

Day 9

I've Got My Eye On You...

"Behold, the eye of the LORD is on those who fear Him, on those who hope in His steadfast love." (Ps 33.18 ESV)

Think about that for a moment.

The eye of Jehovah, "the self-existent One", is on you. He sees you. He sees every moment, every trial, tribulation, and crisis. Why is His eye on you? Because you fear Him and you have placed your hope in His mercy.

The word "fear" in this verse means to revere, to be in awe of God. If we truly understand that God is our Bridegroom, King, and Judge, we will worship Him and bow our face to the ground out of reverence for who He is.

Even as we bow, we place our hope in His mercy towards us. The word "mercy" in this verse is "chesed" and means His "loving kindness". Because we've learned to lean on Him and trust in His loving kindness, He in turn keeps His eternal gaze on us! He is watching to keep us and protect us in times of crisis and need.

Prayer

Father,

Thank You for keeping Your eye on me! Thank you for Your loving kindness and protecting me in times of need!

In Your name I pray

Day 10

A Firm Foundation...

"Now faith is the substance of things hoped for, the evidence of things not seen" (Heb 11:1 MKJV)

Our physical eyes give us the opportunity to actually see the evidence of the material world. We can actually see, comprehend, and grasp. Our natural eyes give us the ability to see the natural evidence that surrounds us.

Faith is, if you will, the "sense" that enables us to comprehend and grasp the things that are unseen and of a spiritual nature; unseen to the natural eye, but present and true just the same. Faith is the foundation of hope.

Faith and hope go together. Those things that are the focus of our hope are also the focus of our faith. Faith is the expectation that God will perform all that He has promised us in His Word.

Prayer

Father,

Your Word says in Romans 12 that every believer is given a measure of faith. Thank You for the measure of faith You've given me! Today, I ask that You would strengthen my faith, that You would firm up the foundation of my belief in Your promises for those things that I cannot see with my physical eyes. I know Your Word is true and that no matter the circumstance, I place my hope and faith in You.

In Your name I pray

Day 11

There is a Future…

"Surely there is a future, and your hope will not be cut off"
(Prov 23:18 ESV)

No matter the crisis. No matter the trauma. No matter the circumstance, there is a future. As you look around in the midst of your situation, you may see others prospering and doing well. You may feel like there's absolutely no way out and it seems hopeless.

Both the prosperity of those around you and the afflictions you are enduring are but for a moment. There is no reason to envy the one and be stressed over the other. It is promised that your hope will not be cut off! The hope of the believer is founded on the person and righteousness of Christ! And as He is the same yesterday, today, and forever, our hope in Him will never be cut off!

Prayer

Father,

There are times, God that I am so overwhelmed by the circumstances that surround me. And if I take my eyes off of You, I see those around me prospering and doing well.

God, I choose this day to hold fast to the hope I have in You. I choose this day to not focus on my circumstances, to not gaze upon those around me. I choose this day to focus my gaze on You. You are my hope and future!

In Your name I pray

Day 12

Hold Tight...

"Let us hold fast to the profession of our faith without wavering (for He is faithful who promised)"
(Heb 10:23 MKJV)

Hold fast - keep secure.

Oftentimes in the midst of a crisis or need, it is easy to allow those around us to persuade us to waiver in our faith, to waiver in our hope in God to rescue us when it seems hopeless.

God's faithfulness should excite us. God's faithfulness should encourage us to hold tight, to keep secure His promises that we've taken to heart. Reflect on those times that you have seen God move on your behalf.

We must, without wavering profess that His promises to us are true and that He is faithful to fulfill those promises in spite of what the circumstances look like. We must hold fast, walk by faith and not by sight.

Prayer

Father,

I choose this day to hold fast to Your promises for me! I will profess Your word over my circumstances and stand on those promises without wavering. I place my trust and hope in You!

In Your name I pray

Day 13

Mission Possible...

"For with God nothing shall be impossible" (Luke 1:37 MKJV)

This chapter in Luke paints an incredible picture! Two women - one barren and in her old age, and the other a young virgin who has just been told by an angel that she is going to conceive a child by the Holy Spirit and He is the Son of God.

Nothing is impossible with God. Nothing is greater than His power. Nothing is greater than His promises to us. No crisis, no trauma, no disaster is more powerful than God. God can and will bring us through any and every situation.

When it seems hopeless, when it seems darker than it has ever been before, there is a way through and there is One who will successfully bring us to the other side of the crisis. Nothing is impossible for Him.

Prayer

Father,

In my weakness, in my time of need, I place my hope and faith in the truth of Luke 1:37. God, NOTHING is impossible for You. You have the ability. You have the strength. You have the power and You will see me through the darkness and into the light of Your solution to my need.

In Your name I pray

Day 14

It is Written…

"For whatever things were written before were written for our learning, so that we through patience and comfort of the Scriptures might have hope" (Rom 15:4 MKJV)

When Jesus was tempted in the desert, He stood firm by stating, "It is written…" In this scripture in Romans, Paul advises us that mercy and wisdom of God are given to us in written revelation for the purpose of instruction. The Word of God is prophetic in its scope, spiritual in its design, and benevolent in its purpose.

As we study and digest the Scriptures with patience, we begin to understand and embrace the comfort that His promises bring to us. We begin to strengthen our faith and trust in the life the Word brings to us. Then, when crisis comes, we are able to place our hope in His word. We are able to be comforted and at peace when turmoil is all around us!

Prayer

Father,

Thank you for Your Word! God, I ask that you give me a spirit of revelation, a spirit of wisdom as I search and digest Your Word! Open my eyes and my understanding that I may take comfort in Your promises in times of crisis and need!

In Your name I pray

Day 15

Wow! Are You Blessed...

"Blessed is the man who trusts in the Lord, and the Lord is his trust" (Jer 17:7 ESV)

It's SO easy to place our trust in people and things. It's SO easy to lean on the people and things that we can physically see. And as we trust in the people and things we can see, touch, taste, etc., we oftentimes end up disappointed or discouraged in the results.

This verse says that anyone who puts his trust in God is blessed. The word "blessed" in this verse can be translated as "to kneel down in an act of adoration". The verse goes on to say that being blessed is a result of man placing his hope (confidence) in God and not mankind or temporal things this world has to offer. The word "hope" in this verse can be translated "refuge; security". Through single-mindedness and faith, we can rest in His security and adore Him for what He does for us!

Prayer

Father,

I place my confidence in You and You alone. I know that because I trust you as my refuge and my security, that I AM BLESSED! I adore you, Lord!

In Your name I pray

Day 16

Have Courage & Wait for it...

"Be strong, and He will make your heart stronger, all you who hope in Jehovah" (Ps 31:24 MKJV)

We have a choice to make in times of trauma or crisis: We can choose to walk in doubt and fear, or we can choose to walk in faith and courage because we place our hope in God Almighty!

Trauma and crisis are hard to get through, especially if it builds day after day after day. In this Psalm, David tells us to be courageous (become strong), to step out in faith and when we do, God Himself will strengthen our inner most being.

The word "hope" in this verse means to wait, to tarry in the Lord. We must remember that in a crisis or traumatic situation, we must willingly choose to step up, take courage, have faith, and wait in the Lord. The God we trust will, by that trust, strengthen our hearts.

Prayer

Father,

I choose to wait in You. I choose to place my faith in Your Word. I choose to take courage in these circumstances and trust and hope in You. Strengthen my heart. I trust You!

In Your name I pray

Day 17

Holding Steady...

"Let Your steadfast love, O LORD, be upon us, even as we hope in You" (Ps 33:22 MKJV)

We can rest assured that we can experience the comfort and benefit of God's steadfast love even as we exercise our hope and trust in Him.

So often, we want to be independent. We want to resolve the issue; we want to lead the way through the crisis. We want to place our hope in our own abilities and wisdom. We start strong, but then we waiver, we lose hope and get discouraged when things don't go as we planned. If we would just learn to let God's steadfast love, His kindness, His mercy envelop us and seize hold of the promises He's given us in His word, we would have the comfort of knowing in times of crisis that as we place our hope in Him, He will not waiver, He will not be unsteady in His loving-kindness towards us!

Prayer

Father,

Let Your mercy, Your loving-kindness, Your steadfastness surround and immerse me in all that You are! I place my hope in You.

In Your name I pray

Day 18

Aware of Your Surroundings…

"But since we belong to the day, let us be sober, having put on the breastplate of faith and love, and for a helmet the hope of salvation"
(1 Th 5:8 ESV)

As we look at the days in which we live, we can find many Scriptures that point to being in the end times. Regardless of when you think the Rapture will occur, the Day of the Lord is going to happen. Until that day, we live in a hostile world. The Apostle, in this verse was giving us a battle plan on how to survive when trauma or crisis hit as we wait on the return of the Lord.

We are commanded to be soldier-like in our actions. First, be sober - to be alert yet calm in our spirit. Then we are to utilize two pieces of defensive equipment - the breastplate of faith and the helmet which represents the hope of our salvation.

In times of crisis, we must protect our heart. We do that by walking in faith. We must protect our thoughts by staying focused on the promise of salvation through Christ.

Prayer

Father,

Protect my heart in the days ahead. May I be alert and aware. Because I have placed my hope in Your salvation, I can lift my head in battle.

In Your name I pray

Day 19

Can You Hear Me?…

"But as for me, I will look to the Lord; I will wait for the God of my salvation; my God will hear me" (Micah 7:7 ESV)

In times of crisis, it's easy to get discouraged. It's easy to allow the "voices" of circumstances, traumas, and even well-intentioned advice from friends and family affect your thoughts and actions. We have to learn to take our eyes off of these distractions and focus on the One who can truly see us through. Not only must we look to the Lord, we must also WAIT for Him.

The word "look" in this verse means to peer into the distance, to observe, to spy. We have to intentionally look for the Lord in the midst of our crisis. We have to wait on His plan to unfold in His timing.

The most encouraging part of this verse? God hears our prayers!

Prayer

Father,

Help me take my eyes off of my circumstances. Help me focus on You. On Your Word. On Your promises. I know you know my voice and that You hear my prayers! I will wait for Your plan and Your timing to unfold because it is exactly what I need!

In Your name I pray

Day 20

One Day Soon…

"He will wipe away every tear from their eyes, and death shall be no more, neither shall there be mourning, nor crying, nor pain anymore, for the former things have passed away" (Rev 21:4 ESV)

What an incredible promise!

There is coming a day when there will be no more suffering, no more pain, no more tears, no more trauma, no more mourning, no more death and God Himself will wipe away our tears!

As Christians, we place our hope and trust in Him to return as He promised. We look to that day when we will forever be in His presence, worshipping, giving Him the glory, and honor, and power! No more tears. No more pain or trauma. No more mourning the loss of a loved one. What a day that will be when all of these things pass away! We can rejoice even now knowing that His Word is true and this will happen.

We will lift our eyes and look at Him, face to face. He will, with His unconditional love, wipe every tear from our eyes. What a promise! What a Savior!

Prayer

Father,

We long for the day! Even so, come Lord Jesus, come!

In Your name I pray

Day 21

Always There…

"The LORD is my portion, says my soul, therefore I will hope in Him" (Lam 3:24 ESV)

It all can be taken from us in a moment's notice. Our freedom to worship, our home in a natural disaster, our job, our savings, our health, our loved one. When crisis and tragedy strike, we must have an unshakable foundation that we can place our hope in. We must have an anchor to secure us in the midst of the storm.

In a time of crisis, we can rest on the certainty that God is with us. This scripture says that God is my portion – I possess Him, He is my allotment. Even though everything temporal around us may be falling away or being taken from us, our God will always be ours! He is always our portion.

We can place our hope and trust in this fact. In the midst of crisis, we can hope (wait on the Lord) with confidence that He is with us and He is our portion. His Word and His promises will not fail us.

In the midst of loss, we will NEVER lose Him.

Prayer

Father,

You are my portion. I choose to be patient and to put my hope in You.

In Your name I pray

Day 22

He Will Quiet You...

"The LORD your God is in your midst, a mighty one who will save; He will rejoice over you with gladness; He will quiet you by His love; He will exult over you with loud singing" (Zeph 3:17 ESV)

Chaos. Trauma and crisis bring chaos. When crisis strikes, it is so easy to become overwhelmed by everything that is going on. Suddenly you are no longer functioning in your "normal" way of life. There is a new "normal" and it can leave you in an absolute swirl of uncertainty and fear.

In the midst of that new "normal" is God Himself. He knows you by name. He is right there with you. He is in your inner most parts! He's in your thoughts, He's in your emotions, He's in your soul and spirit, and He is a Mighty One who WILL save!

This scripture tells us that as we place our hope and trust in Him that He rejoices over us. As we lean on Him, He promises to quiet us with His love. In the midst of chaos and confusion a promise of quiet.

Prayer

Father,

When chaos and crisis surround me, I put my trust and hope in You to quiet me with Your love. Thank You for being there with me, rejoicing over me!

In Your name I pray

Day 23

It's Alive!

"According to His great mercy, He has caused us to be born again to a living hope through the resurrection of Jesus Christ from the dead"
(1Peter 1:3 ESV)

Hope is a living thing!

It has life in itself, it gives life, and it looks for life. In times of crisis, in times of trauma and despair, we can have a hope that is eternal. We can have a living hope because of the resurrection of Jesus Christ!

Think about the disciples. When they ministered with Jesus and saw the preaching and the miracles, their hope was strong and alive. They had hope of eternal life. Then He died. And when He died, their hope almost became completely extinct.

Then He rose from the dead and their faith and hope was once again alive!

Hope is not cold, inoperative, or dead. Because of Jesus, hope is alive!

Prayer

Father,

Because of Your mercy my spirit is alive, born again! My hope in You is alive. It is strong. It is eternal! Thank You for the resurrection power that raised Jesus from the dead!

In Your name I pray

Day 24

Wait for It...

"But if we hope for what we do not see, we wait for it with patience"
(Romans 8:25 ESV)

The word "hope" in this verse can be defined as waiting to be rescued with full confidence and joy. No matter our circumstance, we can willingly wait for God to rescue us from whatever our crisis.

The word "patience" in this verse means to be constant, to have endurance, and to be persistent. It paints a picture for us of someone who cannot be shaken from his purpose.

Police officers, firefighters, and EMS personnel face trauma, danger, and crisis on a daily basis. As Chaplains, we put ourselves in the midst of these same situations. We see, hear, and smell the same things. We know that we can place our hope and our trust in God.

We know that we can stand firm and not waiver in our calling. We know that with patience, we will see our destiny come to pass!

Prayer

Father,

Grant me the patience I need to be unmoved in my calling

In Your name I pray

Day 25

The Big Three…

"So now faith, hope, and love abide, these three" (1 Cor 13:13 ESV)

Out of all the gifts, fruit, and tools God gives us to help us get through a time of crisis or need, there are three things we need to focus on to see us through. The big three.

We can speak every known language to men. We can understand mysteries and prophecies. We can find favor with man or with an organization. We can appear to have the answer to every situation. Out of all these marvelous gifts, fruit, and tools, there are only three things that will withstand. Faith, hope, and love.

Faith focuses us on the divine revelation set before us. Hope focuses us forward on what we can't yet see and waits for the results. Love is the end to which faith and hope are the means. The greatest of these three is love. Unconditional love. God is love.

Prayer

Father,

Thank You for the many tools, spiritual gifts, and fruit that You have given me. I ask that You strengthen me to walk by faith and place my hope in the promises of Your Word. May my faith and hope lead me directly to You!

In Your name I pray

Day 26

Rest Stop Ahead…

"Come to Me all who labor and are heavy laden, and I will give you rest" (Matt 11:28 MKJV)

In this verse, the word "Come" means "Come here, now!" Jesus didn't say, "Come to Me when you get your act together", or "Come to Me when the crisis or need is over". He said, "Come to Me now!" This call to come is for everyone. This verse says ALL that labor are directed to come.

With crisis comes exhaustion, weariness, and fatigue. These things can and will weigh us down if we allow them. In the midst of our labor and desire to get through the crisis, Jesus offers all of us a place and time of rest. He literally is saying, "Come to Me and you can cease laboring and take time to recover and heal".

What a tremendous promise! Rest. Being able to lay down the weight of the situation and rest in Him.

Prayer

Father,

In the midst of laboring to get to the other side of crisis, I hear You calling me to "come here, now!" Allow me to keep my eyes fixed on You and draw near to You. I trust in You and I believe that as I lay down my burden and cease laboring, that You will give me rest.

In Your name I pray

Day 27

Waiting Patiently...

"But for You, O LORD, do I wait; it is You, O Lord my God, who will answer" (Psalm 38:15 ESV)

In this particular Psalm, David felt as if he'd been forgotten by God and so he reminds God of his afflictions and complaints.

So often in a time of crisis, in the swirl of chaos and confusion, we often feel that God has forgotten us. We don't hear His voice and we don't feel His presence. As the circumstances begin to envelop us, we cry out to God and remind Him of what we've been through and what we're going through, just like David did.

In the midst of his of his confessing and complaining, David does exactly what we need to do in our time of trouble. He prays for God's presence and help.

Prayer

Father,

I know that there are many times I come to You full of confession and complaining. I know that too often I allow the circumstances around me dictate my words and actions. Forgive me. God, I ask for Your presence and for Your help in seeing me through this situation.

In Your name I pray

Day 28

Forget About It...

"But one thing I do: forgetting what lies behind and straining forward to what lies ahead, I press on toward the goal for the prize of the upward call of God in Christ Jesus"
(Phil 3:13-14 ESV)

God has a call on our lives. Part of that call is serving as a First Response Chaplain. As we progress through our lives and through our callings, we tend to rely on past experiences, good and bad, to formulate current situations. That's not necessarily a bad thing, but too often we refuse to let go of those things and we lose our focus on what lies ahead for us in our calling.

No matter our past, good or bad, no matter our present, we must keep our eyes on the prize of the upward call of God in Christ in our lives.

Prayer

Father,

Thank You for the calling You've placed on my life! I ask for Holy Spirit to help me keep my eyes on the prize of my upward call. I ask Holy Spirit to guide me in keeping You first in my life. Give me wisdom and revelation to know which experiences to hold on to and which ones to release!

In Your name I pray

Day 29

Drop Anchor…

"We have this as a sure and steadfast anchor of the soul. a hope that enters into the inner place behind the curtain where Jesus has gone as a forerunner on our behalf" *(Heb 6:19-20 ESV)*

The writer of Hebrews reveals to us the certainty of God's promises. With Abraham, God swore by Himself that He would bless and multiply Abraham's family. God shows the heirs of that promise the eternal character of His purpose and His inability to lie. Those two things, and the fact that Jesus is interceding on our behalf at this very moment, give us a hope that should anchor us through any storm.

No matter our crisis, no matter the trauma and storm that we must endure, Jesus Himself has gone before us and shown us a path to where He is: at the right hand of the Father, praying for us! What an incredible promise to build our faith upon!

Prayer

Father,

I hold fast to the truth of Your Word! Your purpose for me will be accomplished just like it was for Abraham! You cannot lie! You promised that You have a plan and a destiny for me - to prosper me and not to harm me! You have shown me the way to be at Your right hand, to be seated in heavenly places. I thank You that Jesus is my Intercessor!

In Your name I pray

Day 30

Not Like the Others…

"But we do not want you to be uninformed, brothers, about those who are asleep, that you may not grieve as other do who have no hope" (1 Thess 4:13 ESV)

As Chaplains, we are often involved in death notifications. We see family members grieving their loss: some with no hope and some that know there is life after life, and they know their loved one is with God.

Just as everyone else in this world, we too will experience the death of a friend, family member, or spouse. Paul provides us with some very sound doctrine concerning those who have died.

Paul tells us, as believers, that we should not be ignorant concerning death. As we embrace time to grieve the death of a friend or family member, we must remember that as believers in Christ, we do not have to grieve like those who have no eternal hope. We have a living hope in the resurrected Lord Jesus, and we have a hope in being resurrected to be forever with God throughout eternity!

Prayer

Father,

Thank you for an eternal hope in the One who conquered death and the grave! Thank You for the promise of being resurrected to be with You forever and ever!

In Your name I pray

Day 31

I'm Watching You…

"Behold, the eye of the Lord is upon them that fear Him, upon them that hope in His mercy" (Ps 33:18 ESV)

Are you afraid of God?

God IS watching you. He is observing you. The Creator God of the universe has His eye on you. Are you afraid of God?

Generally speaking, fear of the Lord is missing in today's Church. It is not common to see people prostrating themselves, trembling in reverence as they worship God. We need to return to that!

As Chaplains, we place our hope in His unwavering kindness every time we go on scene. As we minister to those involved in crisis, to those who are experiencing the worst possible day of their lives, and we see the hand of God move, let us thank Him with awe and reverence at what He's doing through us. Let us worship with trembling the One who is ever-present in our time of need.

Prayer

Father,

Your eye is watching and observing me. May my thoughts, my actions, and my words bring You glory. May I embrace an understanding of what it means to fear You, to bow in reverence to You!

In Your name I pray

About the Author

Kevin Hardy serves as the Executive Director of the Midwest Chaplain Network. He also serves as the Lead Chaplain for the Kansas City, Missouri Police Department and as a Chaplain for the Grandview, Missouri Police and Fire Departments.

Kevin was ordained in 1993 and is currently serving in pastoral ministry at CreateChurchKC in Kansas City, Missouri.

Kevin earned a bachelor's degree in Biblical Studies from Luther Rice Bible College and Seminary in Lithonia, Georgia.

He is the proud father of four children, Alicia, Alaina, Alizabeth and Aaron. He has been married to his wife, Lynelle for 38 years.